Letters to Cadence

by Sherri C. Perry

The Library of Congress has catalogued this edition as follows:
Perry, Sherri C.
Letters to Cadence/Sherri C. Perry

ISBN – 13:978-1535253796
ISBN – 10: 1535253797

BISAC: Social Science/Popular Culture/General

Printed in the United States of America

Dedicated to
the one who sewed my Barbie clothes
and
the one who sewed my dresses.

Table of Contents

Table of Contents

Acknowledgements

About the Author

~

"The proper definition of a [wo]man is an animal that writes letters."
Lewis Carroll

~

"Letter writing is the only device for combining solitude with good company."
Lord Byron

~

"A letter always seemed to me like immortality because it is the mind alone without corporeal friend."
Emily Dickinson

~

"The one good thing about not seeing you is that I can write you letters."
Svetlana Alliluyeva

Letters to Cadence

Dear Cadence . . .

"We often miss opportunity because it's dressed in overalls and looks like work."
Thomas Edison

~~~

LEMONADE

I've heard people say 'you make your own opportunities'. I disagree that always is the case. I think sometimes despite all your effort what you want for yourself or even what you think you need for yourself you will not, cannot, get.

There is an element to living that is beyond our control. We are not omniscient. Certain opportunities may not present themselves because it's not yet their time.

The question is, while you wait on the door to open a crack so you can push it the rest of the way open, what do you do? Do you sit around and bemoan your fate?

Well, there is another saying, common as dirt, but quite valid: if life gives you lemons, make lemonade. Lemonade might not be the million-dollar contract you covet, but it is honest product for honest work.

Let's say you always wanted to be a dress designer. As a child you would carefully cut out paper doll clothes and later sketch designs and then sew them up by hand. Your dolls and your friends' dolls were always impeccably decked out.

But when you grew up, the design school you applied to turned you down. Your second-hand car broke permanently and you had to cut back on your community

13

college courses so you could pay for a newer, tinier car.

You met someone you loved and together the two of you started a family. You got a degree in nursing because it was practical, not necessarily because it was your heart's desire. You began dressing your kids in clothes you ran up on an old sewing machine when you had the time, but mostly you just went to work every day, listened to people complain about their lives and tried not to sound just like them.

One day in the kitchen you read the list of chemicals in the lemonade drink you made your kids and were horrified. Next time you were in the grocery store you grabbed some real sugar and a bunch of lemons that cost you a fortune.

At home you squeezed one lemon after another on a plastic juicer you'd picked up at Dollar General. Your hands got tired and your imagination went elsewhere while you worked . . . *what about dresses, shirts, socks, all bright yellow with a red stripe above the pocket, hem, neckline...* You could see these lemon-clothes as clearly reflected in the dusty window glass as if they were real.

You began sketching designs again, got online and looked up how to enroll in just one course, took a deep breath and decided not to tell your mate how much you were putting on the credit card for this class. You showed up one muggy night in a non-descript building for your first real design class.

The kids got a kick out of making their own lemonade so much they opened a lemonade stand on the curb. (Yes, you gave up squeezing all those lemons yourself pretty quickly.)

You wound up the proud owner of a dress shop you've named Lemonade Red, and you're pondering whether to go national.

No, you won't find the opportunity of a lifetime in a lemon.

Although, maybe . . .

No need to wait on door one. Go for door two. It might be even better. Just don't forget to remember you already have the makings for something grand.

Be grand.

~~~

"Find ecstasy in life;
the mere sense of living is joy enough."
Emily Dickinson

~~~

B.C.

In that vacuum of a moment when the wind flying one direction meets the wind charging in from the other direction, if you are ever blessed to be in that spot, you will notice there is a drop in pressure. Your body forgets how to breathe, only momentarily, and you'll see on one side trees dipping to the north, on the other side trees dipping to the south, and in the middle, where you are, bottomless stillness.

When your daddy was growing up we adults had a phrase we would use sometimes, often with a smile although not always: BC. Before Child. "We used to go the movies every week BC," we'd say. With a smile. Usually. Or, "We kept our car immaculate BC." With a smile. Sometimes. Or, "We never had spaghetti so much BC." With a grimace. Often.

People tend to mark and remember the before and the after. The valleys and the peaks. If they've had a tragedy maybe they'll remember the days before the tragedy. Or if there was a personal triumph they will mark time by saying 'since then'. I find this practice very limiting. I also think it breeds discontent.

Most of our lives are spent living somewhere in between. Sure, I remember a lot of changes when the 'Child' came along but change is not bad or good, it just is. Rather than dividing up your existence between the highs and the lows, take note of the still spots, the times when you got to

17

make your own decisions without consulting anyone. Mark the times when you served the same dinner you had the last four Tuesdays in a row and yet you made it this time with an extra pinch of salt. Remember all those summer days when you woke up slightly sweaty and you went to bed with freshly washed hair. Recall the way your significant other said the same silly thing to you over and over and over and you always smiled.

Life happens while you are waiting for life to happen. Notice it. Hold your breath when the wind is shifting, capture that stillness and take notes. Remember most of all the in-betweens and name them.

"...after all, the best thing one can do
when it is raining, is to let it rain..."
Henry Wadsworth Longfellow

~~~

LIZARD

A very fat but very fast lizard has been my companion now for over a week. It has so far confined itself to the porch or one day, the window screen. I might not feel so neighborly towards it if it decided to come inside. I have named it Harry. It has hairy little feet, you see.

The day it hung on the screen I studied it from the inside of the house and saw that its little feet had toes that were practically whispery. I'm sure this enables Harry to scurry across pavement, rock and grass with lightning speed. I was surprised though. I expected Harry's feet to be more crabby, more grabby.

Your father loved lizards. He would chase them as a boy. When he caught one, depending on the creature's type, sometimes all he was left with was a bit of its tail. Some lizards can shed their tails at the slightest pull, enabling it to escape a predator. I was not comfortable with your daddy bringing home lizards in shoeboxes. The toads and frogs I liked. But not necessarily the lizards. Maybe because they were so quick. How could you know if one escaped which way it would go? Yet, I allowed it.

It was snakes where I drew the line. I don't mind snakes outdoors. But for a boy to put one in a box so he can feed it bugs and bond with it a few days before letting it loose – no.

19

Licorice. Licorice I will not eat. I know some people who love the stuff. They'll eat it in all colors. I have since, as an adult, understood that licorice root can be medicinal. But when it shows up in ingredients of foods I eat, it has the opposite effect. On its own, even, I find its taste unmanageable.

What do lizards and licorice have in common, you may be wondering. Well, neither is my favorite thing in the world but I will put up with both as long as neither lives under my bed. You might argue I have a relationship with Harry, since I did name him. But if a child brought Harry inside, in a leaky shoebox, well, I would have a problem. He could stay, but I would have a problem - sleeping. If someone told me I had to eat licorice in order to be his(her) friend, I would have to broker a compromise. I wouldn't care if they ate the stuff; just don't make me do it.

There are different levels of tolerance. You will find some things make you uncomfortable - in a general way. (Always pay attention to your instinct though. If you feel you are in danger, run.) Some things will keep you up at night. Some things will make you sick. Some things will just not be on your favorites list because you do not understand them. (Those things I encourage you to study and learn from.) But lumping together all those things you don't like for one reason or another, from vague dislike to scratchy active dislike, is that fair?

Even strong dislike should be considered carefully and with clarity; avoid the word 'hate'. How can you hate green beans? How can you hate a temperature? How can you hate, yes, even a snake?

How can you hate people of a different color, religion, orientation, persuasion? This thought is so old we have forgotten who first said it, but people you might think of as books. You should not decide for or against a book based on its cover; it's not enough to say we know all us are different. We should read the 'books' and try to understand those differences.

I am not telling you to not have convictions. On the contrary, you should have convictions about things that matter.

That is called discretion, knowing which things matter enough to stand on one side or the other. As you grow and develop that discretion, keep in mind we were all born with unlimited possibilities. (Probabilities are not the same as possibilities.) If you restrict someone, or yourself, then you limit the connections that make life interesting and in the long run, worth living.

Let's be in the business of limiting as little as possible. Harry would agree. He is sitting in a sunny spot, stupendously still. All of his feathery little toes are flat against the ground. Nothing, absolutely nothing, would move me to move him. He is entitled to his space, his existence, his happiness. As are you. As are we all.

~~

"What happens is of little significance compared with the stories we tell ourselves about what happens. Events matter little, only stories of events affect us."
Rabih Alameddine

~~~

DOLLHOUSE

I am giving you my dollhouse and I wanted you to know a few things about it. It was a project of mine when I went back to college in my thirties to finish getting my first degree. Your daddy was in junior high. I would work all day, go to school at night, come home and get dinner done and help your daddy with homework if he needed any help - and usually he didn't - and then after everyone was in bed work on my own homework.

It was often very late, sometimes past midnight, when I finished my homework and I was too wired to sleep. I would take a paintbrush and open up the paints and paint the dollhouse. I'd had a metal dollhouse when I was little and always wanted a big wooden one, a dollhouse like the real house I would live in if I could. So here it was, and so here it is.

Not everything is paint. You will notice the wallpaper in the dining room. It's made of yellow copy paper and I drew on the flowers with colored pencils. I didn't think to draw the flowers before I pasted on the paper, so I was practically standing on my head to get the flowers done with my big hand and the pencil crammed into such a little space.

Green trim was a decision I wrestled with. I wanted the house to look lively and hopeful, things I was unconsciously wishing for myself. But I didn't want the garish pinks and purples and sea greens I had seen on real Victorian houses. The dark green against the white was both happy and dignified. At least, I thought so.

The door has never closed properly. I will confess to a lie. Yes, Cadence, your grandmother tells stories. I have always told people who asked if I built the house: Yes. Really, it was a model and the design was being discontinued, so the hobby store sold it to me already built.

The door was uncooperative when I got the house. I was not sure how to fix it and as time went by I decided I didn't want to fix it. A door that won't close all the way lets light in and butterflies and roly-polies too, right? Not only bad things come through an open door.

The broken plastic window also came that way from the store. I do know how to fix that, it's a simple fix. Maybe I will do that someday, if you would like for me to. But when I see it I am reminded of when your daddy accidentally broke a window of a vacant house. He was mowing the lawn for the realtor and a rock hit it. He owned up to it, to the realtor. Your daddy's honesty was one of the reasons that realtor liked him so much, and years later when she was in a position to help him in a matter totally unrelated, she did.

Now for the furniture. I bought it when I had any extra money so none of the pieces really match, set to set. The piano represents the pianos your daddy played - did you know he had two real ones in our small house? The little piano is a Christmas ornament so if you want to hang it on a Christmas tree, you certainly can.

The table I bought as a single item because it was so pretty but it didn't come with chairs and I couldn't afford the

24

ones that matched in a separate package. I bought you a few oak chairs when I put all this together for you, but you might someday want to save up your money and buy chairs that match the table.

I have never been much of a cook. You'll notice your house does not have a kitchen. Maybe you will grow up to be a wonderful cook. If you want a kitchen in your dollhouse, we will find a way.

Your dollhouse has a room with bunk-beds. Your daddy had bunk-beds when he was a boy. He loved sleeping on the top. When he had friends over, they had to sleep on the bottom. He eventually got too big for his bunk-bed. But here in your dollhouse, you can keep your play family the same size forever.

On to the business of the dolls. I never bought any for the house. I like buildings, the shape of them. I like rooms, the layout of them, the lines of un-pressured space. I even like furniture some of the time. But I thought, as I worked for months on this house, that people tend to crowd the clean lines of well-built and well-planned buildings. I didn't want doll-people to mess up my house. Isn't that silly?

Your Great Aunt told me once that a DOLLhouse was not really a DOLLhouse without DOLLS. She had a point. The dollhouse was not a dollhouse to me. It was a way to stay sane and calm myself after 20 hour days, something I could control, a pretty project.

For you, though, for you this is a dollhouse, not a project. This is a structure that will fill out and become real within the freedom of your imagination. You need, you deserve, dolls for your dollhouse.

25

To start you off, I've painted some little wooden pegs to look like people. You can pretend they are related or not. You can pretend they are girls, boys, men or women. You will see that I've painted their skin different colors. After all, no matter where we come from, we live in the same world, and in God's eyes, we are all already family.

When you get older I will be happy to buy you real little dolls that will fit the house. Or, if you'd rather, I will help you make your own.

Are you wondering what I did with the house once I finished painting it and furnishing it? I've had the house in my life for sixteen years.

When I finally got my college degree I got a job teaching high school seniors. They were teenagers who came from poor neighborhoods. Many had been in gangs and had seen much trouble, but they wanted to make something valuable with their lives. They didn't live in pretty houses, they didn't, most of them, live in a house at all. What they wanted was to be the best son, mother, father, uncle, doctor, teacher, writer they could be. They studied hard, tried hard, worked hard, and so many made it to college and beyond.

I loved that job. I had to change schools after two years so I could be closer to where your daddy went to school, but I kept teaching and at the next school I taught junior high students. Many of them too came from poor families. I brought the dollhouse one day to class to show them and it stayed.

The children loved the house. I taught English. I gave them a monthly assignment, to imagine a different family in a different time in history living in the house, and to write a

26

"house story" with the house contributing as a living, participating member. Through the years, at that school and the one I went to next, young people have written hundreds of stories about imaginary families living and growing up in your dollhouse.

I read students' stories that had bits of real life in them. I knew sometimes the students were writing about their own lives, their own houses, their own parents and families. When a pet died, when the house spoke to a sad child, when a storm knocked down a tree onto the porch, when parents argued, I knew the child writing the story was writing from his or her heart.

I also knew that when a big sister got married in those stories, or a daddy got a promotion, or a child had a birthday party in the house's dining room and the cake was covered in raspberry icing, that the child writing the stories was again writing from heart and memory. So this is your dollhouse, ladybug. It is a storyteller house that tells some of my story, some of your daddy's growing-up stories, and holds in its spaces stories of so many children you will never meet. It has plenty of room yet for your own stories.

Have fun with it. Re-paint the house if you'd like. People it with families. Draw on the walls. Be happy.

Live big. Set dolls on the table if you don't like the chairs. Tie balloons to the chimney. Don't be afraid, in play or for real. You have family all over the world, family you will never meet, family who dream and hope and imagine just like you do, connected to you by your shared humanity.

And there will be things in your life that you will want for what seems like forever, and those things won't come to you. You will understand someday that, like the big Victorian house I thought I wanted all my life, really you just wanted the idea of that thing, the essence of it, or maybe just a model of it.

You may find as you start telling your own life stories that the only thing you can control are the endings. Our beginnings we inherit, our in-betweens we sometimes have to compromise due to detours or contingencies, but our legacies are ours to imagine and construct as we like.

How you and your house live your life, what you put into your life for other people and not only and always for yourself, will come back to you in the end. You will be blessed with the right paint color, a front porch, a broken window, color-penciled wallpaper, a set of bunk-beds, and an open door through which butterflies will float and pill bugs will roll.

You will have a house and a life that will be treasured.

"The cure for loneliness is solitude."
Marianne Moore

~~~

WET AND ALONE

It's misty and cloudy tonight, drizzly, with distant lightning. No, this is not a weather report, circa March 27, 2014. I just watched a movie, 'Young Victoria'. There's a scene where it's raining, as I understand it does almost constantly in England, and Prince Albert asks his new bride and queen: is it always this way? She laughs and says yes. They wind up in the rain, embracing, the most powerful woman in the world and her prince.

Yes, they're often in the rain, these romantic scenes, and it seems they usually end there. On my balcony here off the fourth floor I stepped out to see the weather once the movie was done. It's dark. It's been a long week at work and your grandpa is there in Oklahoma with Snickers, his dog, for your birthday, so it is just me and Bob the Cat. I am not lonely though, and this is what I want to tell you.

Your father and I, when he was small and growing bigger, would sit regularly on the porch of whatever house we were in during so many storms. We would stick out our legs into the rain and then pull them in again, shivering and mesmerized, watching it pour, watching and guessing how much dry space we had left on the concrete until the damp got underneath us. We were together, your father and I, but unlike the raindrops that run into one we were not the same, we were different, and we were, as we all are, inside ourselves alone.

When your dad was in high school his counselor said admiringly of him, "I watch him cross this campus, from my upstairs office window, and he often walks alone, but he is never lonely. The boys come and go to him, talk to him and walk alongside him and then leave. He never alters course, he never follows them, he just keeps walking, with himself."

I liked how the counselor said: "walks with himself." Alone, yet not lonely. In your life perhaps there will be an evening that you find yourself watching a romantic movie on whatever device you'll be watching movies on in the future, and the night will be dark and there will be distant lightning. You may think to yourself: I need to text somebody or call someone or conjure up someone out of the dark from an electronic cloud to talk to me.

Don't do it.

You don't need to be afraid or even reluctant to be alone because alone is good. Trees grow best and tallest with space. Alone, you'll get to decide for yourself what that movie means to you. You'll get to watch uninterrupted the rain smatters and feel unimpeded the wind. You will get to decipher whatever cloud you want. You will get to step outside and in your bare feet, on rough boards of a fourth story balcony or perhaps on a damp concrete porch only four inches up, and no one will tell you not to get wet.

Try to make it happen that the space outside you and around you is bigger than the space you live in, so when you are alone you will have a small physical space to welcome and keep you when you return, a complement to your secure inner space. And while you are looking around, note who you are and who you are made to be.

Of course, you may fall in love with someone who loves you just because you are who you are, not because you are a princess or a queen or a CEO or an artist or a very poor but very determined author, but because you are you. Like Queen Victoria, you may someday recognize one who loves you and then you will decide on your own whether or not you want to become two. That decision is not a mandate, despite what your immediate heart may advise you.

Meanwhile, go out of your way to stand alone in the rain. Rain is meant to clean and re-create life. Lightning is light. Put your bare legs out there, breathe the electric air. You are alive. May you never be lonely, but my hope for you is that you may often be alone with yourself.

~~~

~~~

GRATITUDE

There is a popular actress and TV host who has made big money off reviving the ancient thought of gratitude. For years she, and others in the public eye have exhorted Americans to be thankful. I fear that we have grown immune to all the hype, which is sad because being mindfully grateful can indeed transform.

Currently I have a deep blue canister on my desk at home and a small pad of paper in front of it. Every night before I go to bed, if I remember, and I remember the majority of the time, I'll tear off a piece of paper, date it (I find some days I have to hunt through my memory or calendar for what day it is, that's how fast time can go when you are not paying attention) and I will write down something that happened that day for which I am grateful. I'll fold it into fourths and pop open my canister, which used to hold fancy coffee decades ago, and push it down into the rest of the paper nest.

This is not original with me, the gratitude jar. It became a 'thing' a couple of years ago and via social media every new year people start talking about it again. The idea is as the year progresses and certainly as the year ends you will have a visual confirmation of how much you truly have to be thankful for. In the words of a negative thinker: how much your life really does not suck (pardon the phrase).

My blue canister is not see-through so I am not following along exactly how my collection is growing but I look forward to the end of the year when I can dump out all the little pieces of paper and read back about things in my life for which I was grateful.

I am finding something out about myself though, as I go along. When I write down what I am 'thankful' for often I am simply writing down what was good about that day. I realize as I'm writing that I did indeed recognize that something good happened or that I did something good or that someone else did but I did not recognize at the moment that I should have been happy about it.

Gratitude in hindsight. Which is probably the whole point of the exercise. Better thankful later than never.

You have been trained, as have most children, to say 'thank you' when someone gives you something or when you want something and you want to appear appealing. We say 'thank you' so often it loses any meaning. Although saying it is important for the exercise of saying it - and in saying, perhaps making it true - often saying thank you is an empty gesture.

I am even hesitant to encourage you write down your gratefulness or to mark your emotional response when something good occurs, because writing can become rote and feelings are not dependable.

So what then, is the best way to experience and express gratitude?

True gratitude brings with it action. When you are truly thankful for a sunny morning or an attentive friend or a new adventure or grateful that you got to experience a painting or hear a symphony, you will want to share.

Noticing that you are benefitting from a force not your own is the first thing to do. So many of us go through our lives not noticing much of anything because we have deadened our senses with too much of everything. But once you've noticed a good thing, then try to share.

No, you cannot share a sunrise if you don't happen to have someone sitting right there next to you. But you can take that uplift of spirit into your classroom and smile at another human being - even your teacher. Teachers appreciate smiles. So do bosses.

You can take the thought of that painting that you sat and studied in the museum the day before and translate it to picking up a small bunch of flowers at the market that afternoon and surprising someone at home.

You can take the news that you have been hired at a dream job and instead of telling the next fourteen people how awesome you feel about this development, listen to them describe their day and participate in their feelings.

We usually have so much joy to spare we could share it with dozens of people everyday, and that would not only make them happy but make us deeper, happier people too. But we don't do it. We grow miserly with happiness that we truly, in most cases, don't deserve in the first place. Happiness is grace, after all.

Grace occurs when you have done nothing to deserve goodness but goodness comes to you anyway.

So I will go ahead and encourage you to say, write or share your thankfulness even though it might become rote. A habit is good to have when all else fails and your world seems to be falling apart. Go ahead and remember that you have a habit of being thankful, of recognizing grace, and even when you don't feel like it, fill out a piece of paper with the date and write down what undeserved goodness has come to you that day. Even if all you can come up with is 'I am still breathing', that is not only enough, that is glorious!

In thankfulness for the person that is you.

"The reason birds can fly and we can't is simply because they have perfect faith, for to have faith is to have wings."
J. M. Barrie

~~~

TAKE FLIGHT

Years ago when your great-grandmother - your PaPa's mother - had her family over to her house in the country she would take your daddy and me for walks. We would watch her veer off paths and into grasses and woods for the sake of stroking a leaf, naming a bird, observing a bug or expounding on the long-ago value of a particular weed to settlers.

The bird-watching caught. Your daddy was in Scouts and bird-watching was a badge but even before we started watching and trying to identify birds for Scouts we were doing it for fun. There is value in knowing what to call a certain bird. There is value in knowing what the bird eats, from where in the country or the world that bird is the happiest or originated. There is value in looking up in the sky and seeing the underside of a bird and knowing from which family of birds that shape hails.

There is always value in knowing, knowing anything. But the knowing should not be the end goal. Watch birds for their magnificence. Birds are a favorite variety of knowledge to me, and I think to your daddy too, because birds can do something we humans can't but have always wanted to. They fly. They don't start out as babies knowing they can. They watch their parents and eventually fly

37

because they think they can do it too.

Yes, you can fly in an airplane, or on a glider, or maybe you'll fly someday in a hot-air balloon or with a jet pack. Maybe you will go to another planet on a ship and float weightless in space while you perform a repair mission. But to fly I suspect humans will always have to have mechanical help.

Birds only need their wings.

I saw a movie once, *Maleficent,* where a powerful fairy had her wings cut off in a brutal manner by an enemy she had thought was a friend. She could do all sorts of magic, and she did, but to grow her wings back was beyond her. Her wings lived on, in a box in her enemy's castle, waiting to be reunited with their owner. But she could not grow new ones. She had been given one pair of wings, and one pair of wings was all she would ever have.

I still carry a pocket-guide of common birds in my car's glove compartment. (By the way, have you ever wondered why that space is called a glove compartment? I'll save that for another letter.) I still try to notice and look up at the birds that soar over my head.

When I go visit a certain cemetery out in the country - not because I know anyone buried there but because I like the special combination of the wildflowers and the hawks - I will try to name as many songbirds and birds of prey that I can. The birds are truly free. The big ones will capture updrafts and float, expending no energy whatsoever. The little ones will flap energetically from flower to flower, tree to tree. None of them ever have to come down from space and sit on my head because they are tired or bored or forgot what it was they were supposed to be doing.

Spaces free of people and their problems may be shrinking even faster than they are today when you are grown, and so I encourage you to join forces with others who understand the value of preserving what's left of nature. Even now, in 2014, we are losing our honeybees, an ecological disaster in the making.

But once again, I digress. Get a field guide, find a field, go bird-watching. When you are feeling tired or aimless or confused, add to your repertoire of knowledge about birds. Your Nanny, what we called your PaPa's mother, would be so proud of you. And if you feel a yearning to also learn what to call that roadside weed or that towering oak or that bug that skitters over the tops of ponds, you will be keeping a tradition alive.

~~~

"A single rose can be my garden . . .
A single friend, my world."
Leo Buscaglia

~~~

FRIENDS

One cannot underestimate the value of friends. There is a saying, and I am paraphrasing it badly, that some friends are meant to be yours for a day, others for a season, a few for a lifetime. I have seen young people often make the mistake of thinking a friend for a day or a season is someone they own forever. There are two problems with that.

No one owns another.

Very few friends are meant to be forever.

I never got the hang of friendships very well. When I was growing up, because of various things going on in my family, friends were not something that were encouraged.

As a result, as an adult I would sometimes deny long-term access to a person who should have been my friend for a season, or try to build a lifetime around a friend who was supposed to be one for a 'day'. I will never be perfect at this balance, no one is, but I've gotten better at it.

I do have one bit of wisdom to share about friends. Like the color wheel, where colors way across from each other work well with each other, accept and nurture friendships with those very different from you while you also accept and welcome friendships with those who are practically a mirror image.

What is the best way to have diversity in my friends, you might wonder. You might be in a school where

41

practically everyone has been together since kindergarten. Your besties may be from families your parents have known forever. It may be hard for you to see, notice or locate friends who have not been around since your time began.

But I hope for you opportunities to reach out. Maybe there will be a choice between two sports teams, one at school, one in the neighborhood. With your parents' input, maybe you can choose the neighborhood one. One day there will be a choice between an elective with people you think you have a lot in common with and another elective with people you don't. Choose the latter.

Just because someone works in a job you never thought of as desirable or sustainable doesn't mean that person wouldn't make a valuable friend. Just because a person might like one kind of book and you another does not mean you can't develop a rapport.

Obviously we want to surround ourselves with people who desire and work for a healthy and positive world. It's inevitable that you will connect with people who seem to drain the very air everyone breathes and you might be inclined to rescue them, whether they asked you to or not. Help only as far as it doesn't cost you your convictions or well-being, and then move on. Good friends are like hardy plants. They do need watering and care. They should not require daily tending.

Your father has had a best friend since he was in elementary. Their first real connection was in second grade over a foot race. Your dad wanted to beat his friend in the worst way. Around and around the little track they ran. (If memory serves correctly, your dad did win.) They will be

42

the first to tell you they have not always agreed on things and there have been instances where they took a break from each other. But they always came back to the friendship.

I believe that you will find a few truly good friends who have the freedom to come and go and yet always come back to you as a confidant, a friend meant to last. One, two, maybe three of these is all you need. Be kind, be a listener, laugh a lot. Gather people around you who feed your soul and whose souls you feed in return. Be varied and open-minded. Just as we need a balanced diet, we need a balance in our friendships.

And never forget, friends may be your lifeline when even your family is not. I have found that also to be very true.

May you be enriched with true love and friendship.

~~~

*"There are things known and there are things unknown,
and in between are the doors of perception."*
Aldous Huxley

~~~

PIECES OF A WHOLE

Jigsaw puzzles would often sit on our dining table for weeks when your father was growing up. He says he never liked working them but he used to sit with me for hours looking for the right pieces.

I haven't worked many jigsaws lately. I tell myself I don't have the time or patience, and maybe most days I am right in that. I do work jigsaws online. There is a very satisfying 'click' when one gets a correct piece on the computer version.

When you are grown you may not have the luxury of doing much by hand anymore. Most of your business and entertainment will probably be on screens or in some sort of virtual space. If there are real-time opportunities, you may have to seek them out. Satisfying clicks aside, there is a gratifying connection between mind and hand that makes puzzles on a table ten times more fun than puzzles on a screen.

For fourteen days I will be by myself on a mountain in southern California, no internet or TV, supposedly writing diligently for hours on end. I am currently on day four. I will tell you honestly, I do as much sleeping, eating, staring at the horizon and reading as I do writing. I am also working a real-time jigsaw that I brought with me. In case I get bored, I told myself.

(I wonder if a writer getting bored with her own

45

writing is an omen for a bad commercial outcome?)

But as I have been working on the 500 piece jigsaw two things have come back to me that I used to be very aware of when your daddy and I worked on them together so long ago.

Time.

Perspective.

When I haven't moved a piece successfully for many minutes I tell myself to get up and leave it. I don't always listen to myself, but when I do I find I invariably land a piece almost immediately when I return. A brain can get stuck. I'll try to fit the same piece in what turns out to be the same spots and in the same direction over and over and over again. When my brain gets a break, though, I come back and remember what I've done that didn't work and I try something different.

Which brings me then to perspective. I'll sometimes walk around to the other side of the table and look at the whole job upside down. I'll take individual pieces and turn them four ways – something you think you would remember to do, so obvious, but you don't - and sometimes I will even look at the blank backside of a piece. Colors and lines can confuse the brain. Really, all the brain needs sometimes is a shape.

I know you are way ahead of me. Jigsaws equal life. Puzzle pieces are like real-time problems. Yes. They are. Take your time when you are making a decision. If something is not clear, don't force it. Walk away from it. If you can afford the time walk away for a day, a week, a month. If you can't afford the time, walk away for a minute.

Get a different perspective. If your brain is so stuck seeing a situation one way then ask a friend to look at it with you. Different people see things differently. Pull your mind's eye way back so only the shape is what you see. Freeze a group situational picture in your mind, soar above it, circle all around it. Turn the problem around to theoretically be someone else's - now what does it look like? Think up the most upside down, backwards solution and then seriously consider that solution.

Time.

Perspective.

I wish for you plenty of both.

~~~

" "Take some more tea," the March Hare said to Alice, very
earnestly.
"I've had nothing yet," Alice replied in an offended tone,
"so I can't take more."
"You mean you can't take less," said the Hatter. "It's very
easy to take more than nothing."
"Nobody asked your opinion," said Alice."
Lewis Carroll

~~~

TEA COSY

Let's talk about tea. I was going to say that you probably don't drink tea yet, but you do. You are constantly clamoring for us to put sweet tea in your cup.

I hope tea is still around when you are grown. When you drink tea you are drinking thousands of years of history. It's been around that long.

I am aware many things that are here now are on their way out of existence. Radio, for instance. One would have thought that radio would have died before now, considering all the devices people have that will play music, communicate the news instantly, entertain, amuse, keep them company. I have had the occasion recently to only have the radio and nothing else, because where I am - imagine this - internet signals and television signals don't reach. I did not know so many interesting people still populate the radio waves. The world is not so small that I don't get a tiny thrill when I hear the announcer say the station originates in Los Angeles, a place I've only ever driven around on a freeway, never been in.

But back to tea. In the South we drink it mostly iced.

49

There are flavored teas. If you walk into the grocery store you may still be able to find half an aisle devoted solely to different brands and flavors of teas. I recommend the peach flavors, or vanilla. (Peppermint is good when you're sick, mostly because as you drink it hot it permeates your sinuses. Yes, drink tea hot too. More on hot tea later.) There are all types of tea, from all around the world. Experiment.

Iced, perhaps with a sprig of spearmint leaf on the side of the glass, is for sipping, not gulping. Iced tea is supposed to remind you of wide porches and summer breezes, even if you've never been on a wide porch. Don't get stuck in the morass of a sticky truly southern summer afternoon. Elevate yourself, along with your iced tea, to a higher frame of mind than reality dictates.

Get a pretty glass. Real glass, not plastic. Save the straw for when you're at a fast food drive-through and want to drink what they pass for tea. When you are relaxing with iced tea, consider the glass, the ice itself, the color of the tea when you hold it up to a window that's letting in the late-afternoon sun.

Then take your tall, pretty glass with its amber tea onto a porch. Locate the rocking chair. Slowly, so you don't spill the tea, sit carefully and hold the glass on the arm of the rocker. Sip occasionally, letting the tea linger on the back of your tongue, where your mouth is the hottest, and then let it cool your throat in bright happiness.

That's tea, the way it's meant to be taken, seriously but with a smile. Of course, in the world I live in and the one you will probably live in this is not how your iced tea will be taken. You'll be up late one night, studying, and pour a glass straight. Or you'll be in front of the television or computer and finish a glass without noticing that you'd even begun one. To save your teeth from staining you may make a habit of always drinking with a straw.

The odds of you drinking the iced version on a veranda are slim, I know. The odds of you drinking hot tea from an antique cup with a slightly crazed but still solid saucer are also slim. But I will wish these things for you. When you inherit my teapot collection, imagine me drinking tea from everyone one of them - although, in truth, several are unsafe to drink from because of lead in their paint!

As for the hot tea, it needs to be hot. Hot tea, antiquated as it may sound, is even better at connecting a person to her world than coffee is. I drink coffee, I like it very much. I pretty much cannot wake up and function as a decent human unless I start my day with several cups of coffee. Coffee is what reminds me I am meant to be human.

But tea, well, tea reminds me it's worth it, being a human.

If you like it sweet, buy a flavored tea, but I advise you not to bother with sugar or honey. Such things muddy the tea. Pair it with a sweet cookie and you'll have dessert.

Tea is above all about clarity. Nothing, surely not the tea itself, should be cloudy when you are drinking tea. Hot or iced, bagged or leaves, be sure you have several varieties in your pantry at all times. Tea is patient. It can bide its time, for months if need be. In whatever form you take your tea, it will wait, quietly and confidently, until you need it. Tea is good for getting calm, for focusing thoughts, for soothing a scratchy throat or a scratchy day, for giving you a sense of

51

history and belonging.

I think, as I close this letter, I will start the water for a nice cup of chai. Cheers!

"A man should hear a little music, read a little poetry, and see a fine picture every day of his life, in order that worldly cares may not obliterate the sense of the beautiful which God has implanted in the human soul."
Johann Wolfgang von Goethe

~~~

BEAUTY

Beauty is discussed at length by different philosophers and I am not aiming for a philosophical letter. I do want you to realize early on what you consider beautiful. Whatever is beautiful to you, try to have it in front of you as often as possible, or its best facsimile.

I like to hang beautiful images on my walls. I don't have much money so I can't afford original paintings but the prints and photos I display are beautiful to me. I also like to go to the museum of fine art and just sit on their artfully placed benches to study and take in what I consider beautiful.

What nature gives us is way more beautiful than anything we can put on our walls. That's a beauty we should not neglect either. Nature's beauty is constantly changing, showing us new edges, fresh colors, frayed bits and complex patterns. The beauty we can put in front of us every day, on a wall or on a desk or on a screensaver doesn't have to change as often as nature. It can be an intermittent constant, a touchstone.

What you may consider beautiful might not be what others would think of as beautiful. That's okay. Your dad used to have a dream-catcher weaving on his wall when he was a teen, something his grandmother gave him. I don't know if he thought it beautiful, but he thought it noteworthy enough to look at everyday.

I like letters. Before I knew what fonts were, I was noticing the different outlines of letters. I knew how in some books I read the letters looked one way, and in another book, another way, defined by curlicues or lack of, by thickness, by stems, by waves, by the width of the spaces outside and inside a letter. These things are beautiful to me.

Photographs are beautiful to me. Textures are beautiful to me. Quilts are beautiful to me. I love patterns. I also love architecture. Many of my photographs are of architecture; the cover of my first book is an architectural photo I took. Once when you and I were walking outside my apartment you looked up at a tall building and up, and up, and pointed. Big building, you said, and I said, it's pretty, isn't it, and you said, I know!

What you find and notice and treasure in nature you might find in small pieces and smatterings inside as well. Humans try to duplicate what they find in nature and there are times when they come close. Maybe you'll see the sun in a design, a butterfly in a doll, a cloud in a paint color, a branch in a linear print.

Over the nine months I carried your father I saw six rainbows. I still think they were a sign that your daddy was destined to be a unique and influential individual – yes, I am a bit superstitious. Years later I saw another rainbow build its arch across the sky until it landed smack in the middle of the Mississippi river during a light rain while I was eating in the dining car of an Amtrak train.

Have I been able to bundle up rainbows and carry them in my purse? Of course not. Have I continued to be struck by their mysterious beauty because they hang on the walls of my memory? Of course.

Nature gives us color and you can bring the beauty of color inside. Sorry if I sound like a television commercial. But when it comes to paint, you may decide someday all you want for beauty in your living space is a wall of your favorite color or colors.

I also find floors can be beautiful. For awhile your PaPa and I lived in an old building that had been converted to apartments and the floors were original. I took such good care of those floors. The color of the wood was warm and precious. You will see in photos of your first Christmas you are sitting on that beautiful old floor. What a treasure it was.

There is beauty to be found in the unlikeliest places and pieces. Your aunt gave me a woven combination shoulder bag and cell phone carrier. It's small, has a long black string for a handle. It's the vibrant shades of red that make it so beautiful. I set it out sometimes on a tabletop, just so I can look at it.

You can learn a lot about a person and about yourself by noticing what is considered beautiful. When you have days where nothing happened that was beautiful, be sure you can go home and find something beautiful waiting for you. Be sure you can go inside yourself and find beauty there too.

There is a difference between owning beauty and borrowing it. Putting a permanent stake on a beautiful thing could just as easily kill it as not. Just like you can't pull a pretty flower from the ground and expect it to live forever, you can't always buy or take what you think is pretty and expect it to give you the same happiness as it did in its original state.

I encourage you instead of owning and buying a lot of beautiful things, to invest in a few precious collections and display just a few items in each collection at a time. Rotate them so you see them all eventually but not all at once, since redundancy breeds irrelevancy. For those things that you will destroy if you relocate them, write about them, paint a picture of them, take a photo, or close your eyes and like I have with the rainbows memorize the shape, color, form and spirit of their beauty.

When you can hang beauty on your walls and in your heart, leave space. Don't crowd. Beauty needs room to grow legs and morph into grander, more spectacular forms and instances. Just because you love something doesn't necessarily mean you should own it. Loving beauty might mean you corral it for only a short while and then let it go.

Beauty is in the air you breathe, the stars you see, the kindness of a stranger, the music that makes you dance in the dark. So much is beautiful that you can never touch.

Consider carefully what you are able to capture in your collections of beauty. Let beauty water your mind and grow your soul. Remember beauty is never about jewelry, dollars or possessions. Beauty is about imagination. Beauty is freedom to be.

This letter has mostly been about things, ideas or memories that are beautiful. But everything ever made came from a mind and a soul. The most beautiful person to me is one who listens without judgement, a person who accepts another person as God made that person. I saw a quotation recently by a young poet named Boona Mohammed that read, "If the world was blind, how many people would you impress?" It's a good question to ask oneself regularly.

I hope for you much beauty in the most surprising places. I wish for you the patience, ingenuity and time to find it. I wish for you wisdom to become your own beauty.

~~~

"Knowing how things work is the basis for appreciation, and is thus a source of civilized delight."
William Safire

~~~

NAILS WITHOUT POLISH

When your daddy was maybe five or six we gave him a toy tool belt. He liked to hammer poor ants in the driveway. We thought he might have a mechanical bent (we refused to consider murderous). But he didn't like the toy tools. He wanted the real things. Your PaPa then gave him a junior size but very real hammer and a couple of screwdrivers to tote around.

One day I came home from work to find your daddy had unscrewed all the many parts to his three town toys, what I called the one-piece (I thought) garage for little cars, the airport for toy planes and the fire station for toy people. All the walls, roofs, ramps, doors and varied and sundry bits lay in three piles. Your father had used his real screwdriver to unscrew every tiny screw on those things that he could find.

Furthermore, every electrical plate in the dining room and den had been carefully unscrewed and taken off the walls, placed with their tiny screws lying neatly beside them on the wooden floor.

To say I was stunned was an understatement. My first thought: who knew these town toys had so many screws?! Second thought: who knew the kid even noticed the screws?! And lastly: how in the world are we going to get all this back together?!

Oh, and yes, I thought, thank goodness he showed no interest in poking anything through the exposed electrical outlets. (That would come much later.)

Your daddy put the bigger parts of the town toys back together. Some doors and ramps and screws were dumped into a drawer and forgotten but overall the toys gradually, and generally, resumed their original shapes. PaPa put back the electrical outlet covers.

I didn't fuss at your daddy though. To take things apart has a history with me. I remember I took apart a record player when I was in third grade, to see how it worked, and put it back together perfectly. You don't know what a record player is. But it was a machine that played music and involved a large round moving part that you could see, and a lot of wires and machinery inside you could not see. My third grade classroom had one; every classroom did. I had one at home too, but I wasn't brave enough to take that one apart.

Girls were not considered take-aparters and put-back-togetherers in my childhood. I don't know what I used to take apart the record player but I'm sure I didn't have any real tools. Maybe a butter knife? I guess I at least thought to unplug the thing, or else I would also remember a shock.

So here all these years later my small son, your daddy, was also taking apart things.

I encourage you to do the same. I also, if it's possible, encourage you to search out a hardware store in a small country town that Walmart and Home Depot has overlooked, and see if the hardware store still sell nails by the penny (although you'll probably pay twenty cents per.) My grandpa was a carpenter and before that a tailor. He would take my sister and me to a hardware store and while he conducted grown-up business my sister and I would sort through the various sized nails in the nail bins. If we had been well-behaved our treat was that Grandpa would buy us a couple of nails on our way out of the store.

Little girls back then had no reason to carry nails about in their pockets or small purses but thankfully no one asked us why we did. If asked I would not have had any deep, philosophical answer but I would have told you nails hold things together and that's good.

I didn't build things but I wish my grandpa had taught me how. I did, as I mentioned, take things apart sometimes. I liked to think I 'fixed' things. Through childhood and into adulthood I have often found that taking off a screw or gear or wheel and giving it a good cleaning or greasing and then putting it back fixes things just fine.

If you can't find an independent hardware store where the dust sits like velvet on the shelves and there's a smell of newly-cut wood and turpentine in the air, do the next best thing and buy some plastic blisters of different types of nails, break them open and throw them into a kitchen drawer, all mixed up. Get yourself a tack hammer and a heavy hammer. Google what different weights and sizes of nails are for, so you will know. Buy a how-to book from one of those huge home improvement stores and try to figure out yourself how to build a birdhouse, seal a leaky pipe or install a lamp fixture, before you call a plumber or electrician.

Get yourself a lot of screws too, different sizes. Buy a set of good screwdrivers and wrenches. Keep your hand tools neat, but for the sheer tactile joy of it devote one or two

61

drawers somewhere in your abode just for loose screws, nails, tacks and wires. Run your hands through them from time to time. Can't spare a drawer? Get an empty coffee can - a can, not a plastic container.

Take things apart, put them back together, rejoice if they still work or work again, shrug and sign up for a class if they don't. You'll learn more than the 'how' of things, you'll learn the 'why'. Open lids that aren't supposed to be opened. Push doors that no one walks through anymore. Prop open windows, sit in front of breezes, and study how a window is put together. Don't pay someone to put together that desk that came in parts in a box, with instructions written badly in six languages, before you've tried - for several days if need be - to put it together yourself. Your generation may build great edifices via a 3D printer, but I assure you nothing beats the sound of metal on wood, the squeak of a bolt sliding home true.

As we depend more and more on computers and components so small human hands cannot work with them, let's not forget what our human hands are for. They are for more than holding giant cups of soda or holding the hands of wayward toddlers. Hands are for doing, building, creating, taking down, building again.

Hands are for undoing and putting right.

Have fun taking apart your world.

"Men [and women] seldom, or rather never for a length of time and deliberately, rebel against anything that does not deserve rebelling against."
Thomas Carlyle

~~~

A NOUN AND A VERB

Rebel once in a while. I am not suggesting you ever rebel against the rules of your parents but have you heard the expression "it's a given"? The expression means something is expected because it supposedly makes so much sense.

It's a given that lily pads require water to live.

It's a given that not brushing your teeth will cause cavities.

It's a given that girls want to hang out together and gossip.

The first two are true, but that last one - no, not a given. You can rebel. You can be a girl who prefers to be with just a few, or with one, or with no one. You can be the girl who doesn't talk about people but talks about ideas instead.

I had a very well-intentioned person tell me once, knowing I had been stressed, that it would be good for me to accept an invitation to spend a weekend with several women I knew casually at work, at a cabin one of them owned, and spend the time talking, shopping and drinking.

Other than the obvious, that this person did not know me very well, there was a 'given' implied that I have been rebelling against for a long time. I don't enjoy shopping. I don't enjoy gossiping. I don't enjoy drinking with a group. I, quite honestly, don't really enjoy the company of most women, period. Just because I am one doesn't mean I have to conform to the world's expectation of one.

What was good for me that weekend? Keeping a commitment that meant I was being true to myself.

Did you know once upon a time women couldn't vote? They were considered too fragile, too sheltered, too uninformed, too stupid. That was the given. Someday when you are grown you will get to vote for a president because long ago people rebelled so you could. You may even run for president yourself, again because once upon a time people rebelled against the given so you could.

Rebelling just for the sake of rebelling is not a bad idea either. Keeps you on your toes. Makes you realize other people might have a point. Other people might have a perspective you need to listen to. Rebelling might not mean changing your mind. You might go back to doing or being what is a 'given'. Then again, you might not.

Never run over anyone. Never assume your rebellion is the most important venture or that your opinion the best or the most correct. That's not rebellion. Rebellion, I think, in its purest sense of the word, is deciding for yourself regardless of what others in your same situation are deciding and then matching action to thought.

Why does a sandwich have to mean two pieces of bread? Can't it mean two pieces of cheese with spinach in the middle and no bread?

Why does the woman have to be the one to pick out the curtains?

Why do you have to have curtains in the first place?

You love frogs. Your daddy is rebelling against what is 'the norm'; he takes his daughter frog 'hunting'! Of course, you don't keep the frogs, you let them go. But did you know that you are rebelling against the 'it's a given' belief that all girls are afraid of icky frogs? You are.

Rebel when it matters and sometimes rebel when it doesn't really matter but you just don't want to be or do the usual. Nothing is a given. Keep in mind, the word 'rebel' is both a verb and a noun.

~~~

"Long range planning does not deal with future decisions, but with the future of present decisions."
Peter F. Drucker

~~~

THE LONG VIEW

Until later in life I had always lived in a house that had its foundation firmly on the ground. I knew there were things I didn't like about living so near terra firma: bugs, water, dirt. But until I moved into a high-rise apartment building I didn't realize how freeing living in the air would be.

I don't know where all you will live and I hope you never make that a priority. Deciding that your dwelling has to be the prettiest or biggest or most unique - or yes, even the highest - can take up money and time and emotional capital you should not spend on such things. There are far worthier passions to commit to.

But from living up high for several years now I can tell you this: taking the long view, not just a visual one but a theoretical one, can make all the difference.

Perspective is another way to put it, and I know I mentioned perspective in another letter. But it bears repeating in a different context. Let's consider the hawk. He could sit on a branch every day, same branch, same piece of property, and notice there is a mouse family that looks mighty tasty. (Sorry, but that's the way life is.) If he never left that branch though, if he never left that particular property, if he never soared far and wide and took in a longer view, he would eventually starve. The local mice would run out and our hawk would run out of options.

Hawks don't do that, though. Hawks do have territories to which they return. But during the day they may soar and ride updrafts simply for fun - and yes, years of watching them have convinced me they do have fun - and they range far up and away to hunt.

When you are in the middle of a problem or in the middle of the everyday you may forget to look up or around. You might forget to walk anywhere except around the immediacy of your life. You might forget to notice there are people and opportunities right outside the perimeter of your surroundings. You might forget to even walk, metaphorically speaking. You might just take up sitting.

And that would be so sad. Because the view from up here is marvelous. The view is so big, the horizon so long, the sky so eternal, that you could even experience a delicious shiver of apprehension. (Apprehension is simply anticipation turned around.) You can make more of where you haven't been yet than you can make of where you've been all along. Trust me on that.

Take the long view. Plan not just for today and tomorrow but next week, next year, the next ten years. And be okay with things when plans take an exit or a detour, because believe me, they will. Don't be satisfied with always the same people, the same music, the same food, the same causes. Fill up your mind and heart with lots of long-range expectations and watch yourself grow and expand and accomplish so much more than you ever thought possible.

Come on up. There's room. There will always be room up here.

"Life is about rhythm.
We vibrate, our hearts are pumping blood, we are a rhythm
machine, that's what we are."
Mickey Hart

~~~

RYTHYM

Hopefully when you are grown you will have the rocking chair in which your daddy was rocked when he was a baby. I gave it to him when you were born. Whether or not you have babies of your own, you will love rocking in the chair. Your great-grandfather gave us the rocker when your daddy was born and it fit tall family members perfectly. So many hours in that chair, moving back and forth, back and forth, a slight hitch making it ideal for an infant still used to the uneven tread of his yet-to-be-seen mother.

I notice now that rocking chairs are making a comeback. For years about the only places you saw them were in the nursery department, upstairs tucked into corners of stores, or on old people's porches. But rocking chairs are good for many things not associated with babies or age.

When I rock I can wipe my mind clean. I focus on the rhythm, of course, but other things find their focus as my own life recedes. I can hear the refrigerator hum again. I realize there are birds somewhere on the other side of the window glass. I see small dust bunnies under furniture that suddenly I am content to let sit. If you rock long enough, you begin to notice your own breathing. Your hands fill up with the wide, wooden arms of a rocker, or maybe you'll be lightly holding one hand in the other, keeping yourself for

69

yourself.

I do read in rocking chairs. It's possible but for me not very productive. I get too distracted by not being distracted to stay my eyes on the page. I know some folks sew or work on laptops or talk on the phone but again, the mere action of rocking seems to be more than enough for my mind and soul to handle. Rocking can be all-encompassing.

When you take a rest from your daily life (and I encourage you to take regular rests) I hope you can find a rhythm to your relaxing. You might not be in a rocking chair but be somewhere that is comforting and the same. Differences in the day-to-day will keep you young and sharp but in your downtime it is okay to rest to the rhythm of sameness.

*"After nourishment, shelter and companionship, stories are
the thing we need most in the world."*
Philip Pullman
"The secret of success is constancy of purpose."
Benjamin Disraeli

~~~

A STORY OF STORIES

Let me tell you a story.

Long ago, by your standards anyway, there was a girl
with a little sister. Their mother was inconvenienced by
mothering and so whenever opportunities arose to distance
herself from her daughters, she took them.

Now this little girl would often be sitting in the front
seat of a car with the windows rolled down and be waiting
on the mother to reappear from the store, post office, church
or wherever she disappeared to for hours, and the little sister,
who always sat in the back, was not a patient waiter.

After awhile the big sister would turn and begin to
tell her little sister stories, like she had so often done in the
dark, in her bed, to her teddy bear. Sometimes the stories
involved the adventures of a piece of trash she caught sight
of, skittering around in the gutter. Sometimes the stories
evolved from creepy overtones to cheery endings.
Sometimes the stories had birds and chipmunks as their
central characters. Other times the stories had people for
people and lessons hidden in their actions. Sometimes the
stories were interrupted by their mother reappearing and

never had an ending.

As time went on and years went by the little sister stopped clamoring for a story. The girls began bringing with them stories already printed on the pages of a book whenever their mother popped them in the car, so they would get their stories from authors they would never meet. When stories came into her head the big sister would listen to the stories tell themselves and then would file them away in her spacious mental file cabinet. But when the big sister grew up and had a child of her own - and no, she did not leave him in cars - she began telling stories out loud again.

As they ran errands, she would tell the boy in the backseat about her day, sometimes with irritating bosses, sometimes with wonder-filled Sunday school first-graders, sometimes with dogs or cats or gentlemanly grocers or nosy doctors or fuzzily remembered newspaper boys. The stories were not fanciful but she liked discovering through her son's eyes the humorous or sad or plain weird vagaries of the human soul and human existence, and so she began embellishing the stories with conversations set in different accents, with facial expressions reflected in the rearview mirror.

When the big sister finally went back to college (as an adult and a tired one, at that) and life at home and at work and at school got crazy, there were days she barely had the energy to breathe and she once again let the stories die. Her son had his novels or his schoolbooks and in the back seat he would read or study while she drove here and there. At home they would retreat into their separate rooming spaces, and life went on. She studied, she graduated, and he eventually did the same.

But one day, a year or so after she had gone back to school and accepted that her schedule was going to be impossible for a very long time, her son, who was maybe 12 or 13 and who had begun riding in the front, looked over at her and said, as they pulled to a stop in their driveway, "Mom, you never tell me stories anymore."

She had been very surprised that he had been listening, much less that he liked the stories, and that he missed them astonished her.

She began again. Not so often, not always in the car, but maybe over a quick dinner, or while they pulled weeds, or while they folded laundry, she would tell a story. When he was grown and she was alone she started remembering those stories and other stories that had not died after all, just gone dormant. She began taking the time to write them down. She threw on extra details like you sprinkle parmesan on spaghetti, but at the core was real, honest pasta. Every story, however silly or insane or tragic or joyous it got, whether it featured real people or dolls or real animals or fantastical creatures, had a core of truth in the middle.

This story of stories does have a point. When you recognize a discipline in your life, embrace it. Pursue it. The discipline is not in you to dog you or make you feel beholden. It's in you to enrich your life and perhaps enrich others' lives. A discipline is something you feel compelled to do and that you do regularly. Perhaps your discipline will come in various forms as you change and mature but you will see it for what it is, because disciplines don't hide. And when you recognize it, rejoice in it, because often disciplines turn into magical gifts. My discipline was and still is, telling stories.

I look forward to seeing you hard at work, happy and content, and at peace with your discipline, whatever it is.

"The important thing is not to stop questioning.
Curiosity has its own reason for existing."
Albert Einstein

~~~

TO KNOW

Confusion can be confusing. Aren't we usually sure of what we are seeing, what we should or should not be doing? Yet, confusion will visit, if it hasn't already.

You are a glory. I spent a few days with you recently. Everything is both sure and a mystery to you. If you don't understand something you will pause, think and then say in a sure tone: 'I KNOW.' Never 'yes' to a question, always 'I KNOW.' Mysteries make you pause. Answers make you smile.

Your head will someday fill with too many mysteries and not enough 'I KNOWs' and I can tell you now it is not a happy feeling to suddenly be pulled in several directions and hear a lot of noise you can't escape. You will have a clue to the dilemma of what to do, how to clear through the millions of maybes and coulds and shoulds, but the final solution might not be obvious.

Let's have a story first, before I tell you what works for me.

For years I was about making money. I hardly ever made any but this did not stop me from wanting and planning. I married your PaPa and then immediately quit college - the second time - so I could go to work and earn my own money. Your PaPa tried to dissuade me from quitting school but I was all about making my own way. I did not want any of his help.

75

Now, independence can be a virtue but combined with pride it can be a pit. For years I worked hard and made my own money, never much but enough, and yet I was discontent more than I was not. Things around me went wrong, true, but the source of discontent is always inside, not out.

Your PaPa had a serious medical condition come up, one that had been developing a long time but we didn't know it. The night before his surgery he held my hand and your great- grandmother's hand and told his mother if he died she was to be sure I went back to college and get the degree I was supposed to have gotten long before. She was to be sure, to be SURE I became a teacher, what I was also supposed to become all along.

I'd always thought teaching would pay me too little so even though I knew better I had not pursued it. I had been teaching one thing or another, dolls, pets, your great-aunt, since I was very small and I realized back then what I was made for. I tried to get away from my purpose one more time, after I got my degree, by planning to go into the marketing field. But a clever principal with a bit of trickery up her sleeve got me on the right path to teaching.

The rest is history. I listened to my heart, finally, and it so happened that my heart echoed what those who knew me best already knew.

I still don't make much money, especially compared to what others make with similar experience or education. But I am at peace.

And now back to my answer for confusion.

Listen to yourself. Right now, when you are little and

you are faced with something you are not sure of, you look intently at it. You get quiet, even if for only a moment. Then when you are asked a question, you say in your glorious sure-of-this, no-confusion here, voice: 'I KNOW'.

Will you make mistakes? Will you sometimes think you've figured something out, found your direction, divined your purpose, discovered your one-and-only, built your palace, only to be sent flying smack down on the hard, hard ground? Absolutely. And guess what? While you are lying there sucking up the dust is the time to listen to the voice that hides behind your ear. The voice will have the vital clue about what you should do.

Think back. Think about what you did when you were little that made you happiest. Think back to where you ran when you were hurt. Where, not to whom. Think back to what stories you made up about yourself and your world before you were grown up enough to get confused in the first place.

Clarity shines brightest when there is pain, when there is impending doom, when there is the sharpest reversal. Be brave enough to examine the mysteries. Confusion will go running when you listen to yourself.

And you will KNOW.

~~~

"The greatest fine art of the future will be the making of a comfortable living from a small piece of land."
Abraham Lincoln

~~~

GARDENING

One of the first things I bought you that was not a toy was a little watering can and some flowers in pots. We transplanted the plants into bigger pots, playing in the dirt, and I told you to be sure and water them, they would get thirsty. You were enthusiastic. You had just turned two. I came back a couple of months later and you had loved your plants to death.

"She was real regular about watering them, mom," your daddy said to me, as we looked at the drowned sprigs.

That was okay though. You had discovered that plants are interesting and that caring for something is a good thing to do. My mission was accomplished.

When I was in second grade our teacher told us to bring in seeds, that we would be growing plants. I was ambitious. I wanted to skip the seed part, go right to the flower part. I told my mother I needed to bring in some geraniums and I chose a grown plant with plenty of gorgeous red blooms. I was happy and my classmates were admiring. My teacher, though, was not happy.

"You are to bring seeds," she said. So my mother and I bought seeds. At school I planted a few of my seeds in a cup. Everyone else had a few days on me so theirs grew first. I anxiously awaited my little plants to show their heads. I would very carefully take my cup to the fountain every other day and trickle water on it and I would return it to the same sunny spot on the windowsill.

Finally, one weak little green head popped up and grew slowly on a leggy, equally weak stalk. I was so thrilled! It was like I had a baby! I even named it. I forget what, but I remember I named it.

I thought now I needed to be super-mommy. My plant needed more water and more sun to keep growing. I might have even decided I wanted to overtake my classmates with my superior plant. I'm not sure about that, but it sounds like me.

So I began watering it when I wasn't supposed to. I moved it around a lot, to different windows. My teacher seemed to have abandoned the whole process by then. I don't recall any adult supervision.

And then one day, when I was holding my baby under the water fountain, which was positioned over a large, white sink with a large, gaping drain hole, I turned on the water too fast. You guessed it. My plant swam out of its bit of dirt and its flimsy cup and sailed down into the sink and slurp, right into that drain hole.

My baby was GONE.

I wailed.

Now I was not a crier. My mother made sure of that. If I cried, she 'gave me something to cry for' and it usually hurt more than what started me off. I was an eight-year old stoic. Until that moment.

My teacher thought I had hurt myself. I kept shaking my head no, no, I wasn't hurt, but my baby plant was GONE. Finally, my horrified classmates had to explain. My teacher guided me over to my geranium, still resplendent in its

80

corner of the classroom, and said, there, that will be your baby. It's too big for you to drown.

When my mother picked me up that day she was told the story. She looked at me and in a rare moment of insight said: "Your baby is still alive. It's just growing in the pipes and will someday get so big it will grow out of the pipes and up through the ground and into the play yard. It's not dead at all. It just has more room to grow now."

I have had a garden wherever I've lived. In my classrooms and offices I've had plants. I love growing things. I still tend to over-water. Recently your PaPa told me to please not kill my prized olive tree with so much water. Whenever possible, I sink my hands in warm dirt - ask your science teacher someday why soil is always warm, the answer will fascinate you - and I care for my little plants and cover them in winter and feed them in the summer and prune if I am supposed to.

Gardening is interacting with nature, not just observing nature. Your daddy is growing a vegetable garden as I type. I have friends who not only grow flowers but also fruits and vegetables. What an accomplishment, to coax from the soil your own sustenance! Your great-grandpa, PaPa's daddy, was an excellent farmer and even grew fruit trees. Your Nanny, PaPa's mother, was a whiz at growing flowers and vegetables.

Even if you are living in a tiny studio apartment someday, get a few plants. Tend to them, watch them, talk to them. Yes, talk! You will be a richer person for it.

I know I am. Geraniums remain one of my favorite flowers. (But I very seldom grow flowers from seeds.)
Happy gardening!

~~~

"He that would make his own liberty secure, must guard even his enemy from opposition; for if he violates this duty he establishes a precedent that will reach himself."
Thomas Paine

~~~

FREEDOM

Freedom is a big deal in our country and in our world, and it should be. But I read an article once that made a distinction between 'freedom from' and 'freedom to'.

Long before you were born there was a campaign against drug abuse and the slogan was 'just say no'. Some wise politician (and yes, there are a few) pointed out that if you teach kids to say no to something you must substitute something good for them to say yes to.

Sorry about ending a sentence with a preposition, but there it is, the freedom thing. The article I read was about emerging nations giving their citizens freedom from oppression but very little real rights in return. I thought, the same applies to individuals. We can say no to the bad but we also need the freedom to say yes to something more.

In society we sometimes hear from individuals saying they don't have freedom 'from' something. They don't feel as if they are free from a historical perspective. Those around them may think, yes, they do have freedom from that history; it is history, after all. The real question for both parties is what do those who feel aggrieved have freedom 'to' do or be? Do they have freedom to shop wherever they please without suspicion? Do they have freedom to speak up without being ostracized? Do they have the freedom to dress the way they wish without sanction? No one is saying a person should be free to break the law or hurt another, but shouldn't a person not only be free from his or her past or the past of his or her people, but also have the personal and community freedom to move forward?

The only time your daddy came home from school upset about an injustice was not when he felt he himself had been unfairly treated. He was incensed that a classmate was constantly being teased for something that classmate could not control. Now, I don't want you to think your father was an angel; he wasn't. Ask him sometime about gymnasium electrical sockets.

But in this instance he saw that someone was not free to be himself and your father was angry, rightfully so.

As Thomas Paine says in the preceding quote allowing impediment to another's freedom, even if it's an opponent's freedom, is to ultimately deny the same for yourself.

Listen to another's experience. Open your heart and listen without preconceptions or assumptions. Are they only being allowed freedom 'from' and then are being forced, passively or otherwise, to stagnate without any freedom 'to'? Is it time for you to get angry on their behalf? On yours?

Is it time for action?

"To see a World in a Grain of Sand
And a Heaven in a Wild Flower,
Hold Infinity in the palm of your hand
And Eternity in an hour."
William Blake

~~~

THE LARGER PICTURE

Pebbles. Do you still carry pebbles in your pockets? If not, you should. They are a pain in the washing machine and if they make it through that, then they are a real eye-opener in the dryer.

But they are worth holding onto, at least for a little while. You've heard the saying 'chip off the old block'? Pebbles are bits of bigger rocks, particles of peaks, remnants of rolling thunder and sixteenth notes from the crash of earth's creation.

When you carry pebbles you are one with the larger picture. It's okay to feel small. Small doesn't mean lost. Small just means something has more physicality than you, not necessarily more smarts or potential. When you carry pebbles you are still wondering about life, still have stories floating around in your head about beginnings and why nots and hey, there goes what's-it-called. You are still rejoicing in just noticing.

Your daddy loves rocks. I have always loved rocks. For awhile in my life, geology was the last college course for which I seemed destined to make a passing grade. (Math was beyond me for so many years.) Together, your dad and I would hunt for colored pebbles, odd-shaped rocks, granite with strata, chunks we suspected of being concrete but liked anyway. He had a rock polisher for a couple of years. We set it in the garage because it was noisy, while it tumbled-tumbled-tumbled our pebbles into shiny semi-gems.

Rocks we collected, the bigger ones, would find their way onto shelves or into drawers or cabinets and some finally back out to where they began. The pebbles wound up in corners of floors or under rugs, usually swept out and off the stoop, back into the yard or kicked back to the drive.

All those rocks combined made a past that your daddy and I still share. We still have a habit of not only looking around us but below us, and not always where our feet are going but at what our feet are standing on. I could draw an obvious analogy here but I'll spare you.

Just keep in mind, when you were a toddler you were smart enough to carry pebbles in your pockets. You will always belong to a bigger scheme. Be wise and stay smart. Keep on collecting pebbles.

"For all sad words of tongue and pen,
The saddest are these, 'It might have been.'"
John Greenleaf Whittier

~~~

WHAT YOU HAVEN'T DONE

When you were born I suffered from major regret. No, not that you were being born but that I was where I was while you were being born.

Since I don't truck much with regrets, meaning in Texas lingo I don't deal much in nor have patience for them, the fact that I have a regret about this divine moment makes it important enough to share with you.

I was supervising a middle school speech and debate team at a tournament, which was being held in a large, impersonal high school. I had known for several weeks the approximate date of your birth and then, as plans solidified, the exact date. But I did not make arrangements to miss work and go be with your parents. I stayed put and there I was, my inadequate flip-phone running out of juice, waiting anxiously on updates from your father, all the while running herd on my student competitors.

Your mother had a difficult time and by extension, so did your daddy. This birthing business was of course, new to him, and he was scared. I'm sure your mother was as well. I finally pulled my car around to the front of the high school and plugged in my phone to my car charger so I could get a little more time on the device. Trying to calm him, reassure him, see things through his eyes and your mother's from such a distance was excruciating.

Regret was already pooling at my feet. I didn't tell anyone what was going on; I was ashamed that I had put work before family. For this reason, no one understood why I was disappearing regularly to my car and later to hidden corners and empty stairwells, my tiny phone clutched in my hand.

Shortly before you arrived I was sitting on a cold, concrete step in just such a stairwell, my students in between contest events and blessedly unaware of where I was, and I listened to your near-panicking daddy say 'there's so much blood, mom, it shouldn't be like this!' I cried because I knew nine times out of ten it was supposed to be like this and all would likely be well, but if things were not okay I would not be there to help. He needed his mother, one of the few times your daddy had needed me since he became an adult, and I was not there for him.

You will know regret someday, but I rather hope it is misplaced regret, not regret you deserve to suffer. Few things will make you sicker at heart than to know you messed up and other people suffered for it.

Mistakes cannot be avoided, don't get me wrong. When you make them, though, live your life differently from that moment forward. Life has a way of sending back around what already passed through once, and when it does, do things differently. Nothing can say you are sincerely sorry better than changing your behavior. Some might say regrets aren't worth entertaining since you can't go back in time and change anything. But I think some regrets are worth hanging onto because they can dictate a future course of action.

Of course, you already know things turned out well for you and your parents but I should say it anyway: you were born a beautiful baby, healthy and happy, and your parents, although a little worse for wear, were also healthy and happy. I was not there to share their worry, fear, wonder and joy, and I will always regret that. In the future, though, and there will be one, I will try very hard to be.

May your regrets be few and far between, but may you learn from those that stick.

~~~

"Empathy is the most revolutionary emotion."
Gloria Steinem

~~~

TRANSPARENCY

This past Christmas your dad gave your sweet step-mom a cello. The family was watching with great expectation as she unwrapped her very large surprise gift. Your daddy was filming her reaction; we were all cheering and laughing. I caught sight of your face briefly in between bodies milling about and I shifted so I could more easily watch your expression. Your three-year old face had opened up in awe and wonder and you exclaimed 'a big guitar!' But when you reached out to touch the instrument she firmly but gently told you no. And as she leaned over her new cello, her hair falling across her face, your own face changed. You looked up at her instead with awe and wonder, understanding how happy she was, and you then changed the trajectory of your small hand from the instrument to her hair. You stroked her hair with such gentleness. With a fundamental empathic shift, you became happier for another person than you were for yourself, surrounded by toys though you were.

I caught a glimpse of your soul.

I almost cannot write these words, I feel so overwhelmingly privileged, even in hindsight, to have seen what I did. When humans grow older their souls are often no longer so apparent, their love not so transparent. Humans wear masks and build walls, figurative but very real. They don't open up as they did as children because human adults

91

figure possibly getting hurt is too big a price to pay for identifying openly with another human being.

You do not yet have that fear. You feel another's joy or pain as easily as you feel your own and most importantly you believe another's existence is just as valuable as yours. Cultivate this as much as you can, for as long as you can. Ask yourself when it comes to others: how? What? Why? Still your center and focus on another's eyes. We humans come equipped with insight. Try not to starve it out.

There's an old saying by an educational organization: a mind is a terrible thing to waste. I will paraphrase: a soul is a terrible thing to waste. Let your soul breathe and absorb, dear one. Feel others' souls and your own will be richer for having done so.

"Man cannot discover new oceans unless he has the courage to lose sight of the shore."
Andre Gide

~~~

SENSE OF PLACE AND SPACE

I encourage you to carry maps and dare to get lost. Why should you have access to a map if you are determined to get lost? Well, eventually, you'll want to find yourself and make it home for dinner.

In this age of Google Maps and GPS it is nearly impossible to get lost. Maybe what I am encouraging you to do is explore, find places you've never been. When your daddy was growing up he and I used to set out on Sundays after church. I'd draw a circle on a map as far out as I was willing to drive and he would pick a small town within that circle. He would proceed to give me directions and whether or not I agreed with him I let him be the navigator and I drove where he said. He always chose a place we'd never been. We'd get there, sometimes an hour away, sometimes several hours away, take a picture or two, eat a snack and turn back towards home.

He is not afraid to explore now as an adult. I like to think I played a small role in developing his adventurous spirit.

As you explore, with or without maps, dare to get lost and if you do, dare not to panic. Eventually you will find your way home. And in the meantime, you will build confidence in yourself that you can take care of yourself. I am not telling you to willingly put yourself in blatant danger.

Take a friend or a dog or your phone, or at least leave us a note, but do get out of your comfort zone and do explore. Fear should never control you.

The world is out there for us to see. Close your eyes, pick a spot on a map, then open your eyes and move on out. If you have to, consult the GPS to get home.

But only if you're expected for dinner.

Happy adventuring!

"Learning is always rebellion . . . Every bit of new truth discovered is revolutionary to what was believed before."
Margaret Lee Runbeck

~~~

FACE TO FACE

Some seventh and eighth grade students were discussing technology in the classroom. To my surprise, they thought there was too much. Mostly I was listening, not speaking. I didn't want them to talk to impress the teacher.

Your classrooms may be entirely digital, including the teacher. There won't be many years distant between you as a young teen and these students, though: nine years or so. You may find yourself thinking the same as they do: computers and devices are great for looking up stuff, and phones are good for checking in with friends, but for anything more nothing beats face-to-face.

I did speak up when they were talking about phones: weren't they always texting? 'We only know what to text because we just got through actually talking,' I was told. I suppose that makes sense. Touch bases on the phone, then run the bases in real time.

Their viewpoint that too much of a good thing is, well, too much, extended to the classroom use of e-readers, iPads, laptops and smart boards. 'Most of the stuff teachers do on the Smartboard is just show,' said one. 'I never learn anything new when they turn that thing on,' said another. And iPads for learning are only worth it in elementary, they agreed, saying they themselves only wanted to play games on them.

'We never read out loud in class anymore, we just read to ourselves,' they reminded each other. They blamed that on why they were such halting readers of a script I'd just given them.

Although technology may be required in your classes, indeed even your instruction and textbooks may come from a screen, I hope you'll remember some kids in your not-so-distant past who thought that for all their gadgets, learning was just not much fun anymore if they never lifted their heads and looked around at each other.

Here's to a future and an education that doesn't overlook human faces in real time.

~~~

WORK

Did you know the Lord discusses ants in the Bible? He tells us to consider them, how industrious they are. The Lord puts great store in hard work.

There is also value in being still. In another Bible story appears two sisters, one who takes care of the meals, the visitors and the house, and the other who is content to sit and listen and learn. The busy first sister is told she should be more like the second.

To be busy working or to be busy thinking, which is better? In different times of our lives different strategies are called for. When your daddy was little I would often go in to make sure he was awake in the mornings and rather than getting dressed he would just be sitting in bed in his PJs. I'm thinking, mom, he would tell me. My answer was always: then think at the same time you're getting ready for school.

It was the time in his life to think. Later, when he was older he would work hard mowing yards to save up for things he wanted we couldn't afford to buy him. As an adult, he would work hard in a dangerous job so he could support his family.

I like to think though that while your daddy is working hard, he is still thinking, and not just about his job. He is thinking about why bees buzz or why ants are born knowing they can haul items ten times their size. I know he writes stories - yes, he does, ask him - and I know he remains curious about how things work. Consider his fascination with tornados.

Balance is key. If you start to feel overwhelmed it may be because you have too much thinking going on and not enough work, or too much work and not enough thinking. The ants are good to emulate and the quiet sister is also good to emulate. We listen, we learn, we work, and by matching the action to the need, we can be loving, wise and productive.

I pray for you balance.

"The whole object of travel is not to set foot on foreign land; it is at last to set foot on one's own country as a foreign land."

G. K. Chesterton

"There is no mysterious essence we can call a 'place'. Place is change. It is motion killed by the mind, and preserved in the amber of memory."

J. A. Baker

~~~

ROADS TAKEN

I heard someone say recently people don't remember places as much as they remember what they did in those places. I would disagree.

Your PaPa will tell you I have been a traveler since he's known me. When we were first married I was young and carried a lot of emotional baggage. I was constantly threatening to run away whenever a problem came up. As I matured and figured out your PaPa was not going to run from me and I had no reason to run from him, I instead turned my adventure-starved sights to traveling for traveling's sake.

Not having a lot of money I have been somewhat restricted to going either where it's affordable or where I have friends who will host me. Nevertheless, I have been privileged to visit some of the most beautiful places in our country, and although, yes, I remember what I did in those places mostly I remember the personalities I encountered, personalities of place, then of people, then lastly of myself. Places breathe and have life and potential and they change, and they change us.

You may remember what you do more than you remember the who or the where and that's perfectly good. We are all wired differently. But I want to tell you that at a basic level I believe we all are, at least initially, profoundly touched and changed by what we see and feel, then later by what we do.

I am afraid of water, of deep water. I have never learned to swim. As far as anyone knows I never had a near-drowning experience. I just don't like water. A sense of place has convinced me through the years that although water is to be respected and maybe yes, sometimes feared, water is there to just be. How insignificant a human is, looking out across the Bay from the Bay Bridge in San Francisco! (I prefer the Bay Bridge to the Golden Gate for some reason.) I drive over the water, or I stand on the edge of it, and I mean nothing to that water. I mean absolutely nothing to its depths or to the creatures that populate it. I can sing or tap dance or throw bread crumbs or cry or write a poem and nothing I do impacts the San Francisco Bay.

It, on the other hand, impacts me. Because of it, I have become less afraid, more accepting.

Mountains, rivers, valleys, sky, desert, swamps, palms, firs, pines, sunflowers, ivy, hawks, buzzards, clouds, hummingbirds, lizards, llamas, rhinos, snakes, dolphins, rosemary, sand, jellyfish, waterfalls, coyotes, turtles, deer; I have seen all this and so much more and yet I know that all of it exists for its own sake, not for mine. Our creation story tells us the earth is for us to care for, but do not mistake responsibility for ownership.

100

As you travel (and I hope that some of your travel will be with your Grand), open your heart to the wonder of nature's existence. This might sound odd coming from a woman city-born and raised who loves skyscrapers. But we are allowed dual citizenships. Throw your shoulders back and breathe in deeply. Close your eyes for a bit, then open them. Stretch your arms toward the skies. Be thankful and be simple.

Accept that you are small and your body temporary. It's not a scary feeling, it is a freeing one. Your soul will forever *be*. That is enough, within the vast place we call earth.

Indeed, that is everything.

~~~

"Do one thing every day that scares you."
Mary Schmich

~~~

FORWARD

When you were small a friend of your daddy's was throwing a ball at you. Over and over you missed catching it. It was a big, plastic ball and it would often knock you down. Over and over you stood up and returned it with fury and intent, yelling to stop. But the ball would be thrown again, you would miss again, down you would go again, and bouncing like a ball yourself, up you would come again, just as angry and just as determined to catch it the next time.

Courage means practice. You aren't brave because of just one time you faced down a challenge. You aren't brave because you aren't afraid, because you will be afraid. You aren't brave because you use big words or intimidation.

You are brave because you keep coming back, you keep facing the fear and you don't give up. To be brave means you have practiced doing your best or doing what is right regardless of your own fear or others' disregard.

Your daddy loved to go feed the ducks that lived in a pond near our house when he was young. But the ducks were quite big compared to his smaller self and they were aggressive. They wanted their bread crumbs and the sooner the better. Your daddy was rightfully afraid of them. He would back away from the edge of the pond and they would climb out of the water and dash for him, reaching out with loud, angry, greedy beaks for the bread.

I told your daddy to walk toward the ducks, not back away. When they see you keep coming they know you are

103

not afraid and they'll back down, I said. But, said your small daddy, I am afraid. They won't know that, I explained; all they'll know is that you are coming after them, not the other way around.

Tentatively, the next time we went to feed the ducks, your daddy stepped forward when the creatures became unruly and began climbing out of the pond. They advanced but so did he. He was clutching the bread crusts so tightly they were congealed in his hand. Keep walking toward the ducks, I encouraged him. They will back down.

They did. They finally returned to the pond and waited, noisily, for your daddy to throw them the bread in his own time and his own way.

Walk toward what makes you afraid. I have found that to stop thinking about what scares me, to stop running the 'what ifs' in my brain, to just make my mind go blank is what it often takes for me to override the fear and move forward. I've done this over and over about many things. I'm not talking about being reckless. I'm talking about taking chances that are good ones and that are warranted and taking chances that make you afraid because they are new to you, not because they might destroy you. I'm talking about being brave and having courage because doing so makes you strong and a better person.

Practice being brave. Practice courage. Practice long enough, walk forward often enough, and you will find that you fear less and less.

Be confident in your ability to stand back up and walk toward the ducks. And know that if there comes a time

104

that you can't find that confidence, I have enough confidence in you for both of us.

~~~

"The stupid neither forgive nor forget; the naive forgive and forget; the wise forgive but do not forget."
Thomas Szasz

~~~

FORGIVENESS

Forgiveness is a tough subject to talk about because it is tough to forgive. I will not pretend to understand the concept. There are some things people do that I find unforgivable but I know it is best for the wronged to forgive and so I must be truthful with you. You need to work hard at forgiving, if for no other reason than your own sake. After all, no one is perfect.

I think often folks confuse revenge with forgiveness. I cannot forgive them, a person will say, when in that person's heart is a desperate wish for revenge. I know one cannot wish for revenge unless there is unforgiveness, but I think one can be unforgiving but still not wish hellfire onto a person.

Try to understand in your heart what it is you are feeling against someone who has done you wrong and be honest with yourself. I pray fervently that you will never experience such evil that forgiveness is impossible in your soul, but even if you do encounter such evil, take the long view and attempt what is best for yourself.

Are you hoping for the same damage or worse to happen to the one who has wronged you? If so, that is revenge. That places you in the ranks of those who feel they are entitled to play Fate. Try to move past revenge. You are not all-knowing.

On the other hand, if you find you just simply cannot forgive, then let that be for awhile. Time heals a lot. Do revisit the issue because left on the side of the road unforgiveness can turn in the sun and begin to decompose, poisoning all around. Hopefully, as you revisit your feelings and time goes on you will find the strength to forever bury your unforgiveness.

Forgiving, of course, is what we want people to do for us. If we hurt someone we hope they will see their way to forgive us. Maybe not feel such love for us that they want to be our friend or even be in our presence ever again, but at least be able to hear our name without cringing with anger. What we hope for ourselves we can only strive to accomplish in ourselves towards others.

And another 'of course': forgiving is not the same as forgetting. You may never forget what someone has done to you and remembering can protect you, can remind you, can be instructive. Some of my best epiphanies have come after years of polishing memory and turning that rough stone of memory so many times it has become a shiny gem.

To put yourself in someone else's place, nine times out of ten, is to discover that in a parallel life or circumstance you could have done the same to another. Take that into consideration when you ponder whether or not to forgive.

"When words fail us, music speaks."
Hans Christian Anderson

~~~

CADENCE

Your very name invokes music. Cadence is a beat, dictated by discipline but set free by interpretation. Some of us move wildly to a beat, others of us sedately, but we all move to both inner and outer music.

Even the deaf 'hear' the beat of sound through their fingers, through their bodies.

Your daddy plinked out 'Twinkle, Twinkle' on an old piano when he was three and I, who could read music and played in the middle school band but always wanted the feel of a grand piano under her hands, got excited and decided the boy was a musical genius. Saving and scraping and praying paid off and in a few years we were the proud owners of a Baldwin console. Your daddy went from practicing on the antique upright to a brand-new instrument. I was so excited when I got the call that we had been granted credit for that Baldwin, I hung up the phone and cried.

Hundreds of piano lessons slid through your father's childhood and through our lives, as did, yes, hundreds of dollars for those lessons. Your father, depending on his age and passing temperament, either practiced what he wanted, budding-composer style, practiced piecemeal what his teacher told him to, or protested vociferously at his enforced confinement and simply banged around. We knew he had talent, your PaPa and I, although we understood eventually that he was not Carnegie Hall-bound. We insisted he stick with it until he was eighteen and then he could decide for

109

himself whether to continue playing or not.

We thought we had time on our side. We didn't. When he turned eighteen your daddy closed the piano, moved off to college and except for occasional bursts of creativity on a keyboard has still not returned to regularly playing.

Do I regret insisting on lessons, making him so resentful that he's ignored his talent? Yes and no. I do wish he was at a piano regularly. He isn't and that makes me sad. I also know he still loves music. Tries out different genres on his radio, has no real affinity for any one sort of music because in spite of himself, loves all of it. And he demonstrates a discipline in all that he does that I attribute mostly to all that practicing.

Which brings us back to your name. I don't know why your parents chose your name but I love it. You may end up marching to a unique cadence all your own, and honestly, I hope you do. You may choose to advance along with a group. But whatever form your marching takes I know you have music in you. I catch you catching sounds no one else does. I smile the same time you smile when a TV commercial brings on a tricky tune. I watch you wave your hands, move your fingers and punctuate the notes embedded in the crescendoing ensembles blasted through your daddy's speakers. You spontaneously dance when you hear music, even in the car. I hope that freedom of musical movement is always with you, with a love for sound and an affinity for grace on a breeze.

Start your mornings with music, end your days with it. You cannot do much better than to surround yourself with music. After all, there is music in the birds, the thunder, the rain.

I envision symphonies in your future and parents wise enough to know when to call it quits on the lessons.

~~~

"Human nature will not change. In any future great national trial, compared with the men of this, we shall have as weak and as strong, as silly and as wise, as bad and as good. Let us therefore study the incidents in this as philosophy to learn wisdom from and none of them as wrongs to be avenged."

Abraham Lincoln

~~~

INHERITANCE

You have an interesting line of ancestors watching you. Several sheriffs, some sea captains, quite a few war heroes, a carpenter, a scattering of preachers, more than one farmer and grocer, several teachers, many who were driven by their conscience, others driven by profit, one line who married into local tribes. There are women in your lineage who were settlers and singers and writers. You have some ancestors who lived particularly difficult lives as well, and some who did things you would not want to repeat. I did a genealogy study of our families that took me nearly two years to complete. Although I had always been curious about my family and your PaPa's, I really got serious about learning when I heard you were on your way.

We all want to belong, even those of us who would rather live alone or in a small group. I wanted you to know to whom you belong and that you are a continuance of people who, for the most part, did their best.

I won't go into the stories I uncovered during the study. I have printed the end result and given it to your daddy and several other relatives so I am sure you will read it someday. After all, the project was undertaken because of you. I write now to tell you that history is important. Trite, yes, but nonetheless true, the saying 'those who don't know history are doomed to repeat it'. While that is a negative stance, assuming only bad things happened in history, it is still a relevant thought.

Learn from history. You will be subjected to hours and years of history and social studies in your schooling, so you may think I mean 'learn your history' and yes, that is important. But what I am saying here is learn *from* it.

Experience is the best teacher, that is another common phrase. I never understood why some of us insist on learning by experience even when that experience has been solidly debunked by those who came before us and who left us their accounts of having been roundly defeated. For baking cakes and writing books and arguing cases and organizing campaigns, yes, experience may be the best teacher. But for most of life, if you can find someone who has done it, whatever it is, study them before you embark on your newest endeavor.

The adults in your life are not perfect. Mistakes have been made. Observe, listen and learn. Take the best that's in us, learn from the worst that's in us, and at least try to be original with your own mistakes. There is no glory in history, only stories. Stories build lives and nations, stories destroy perspective and populate politics, stories prove limits and stories blow apart assumptions. Stories expand our horizons and stories shrink our existences.

Stories, and thereby history, are what we make of them. Make wise dealings with history in general and with your personal history in particular, and someday your descendants will remember you for all the right reasons.

Much love to you through the ages.

~~~

"Forget not that the earth delights to feel your bare feet and the winds long to play with your hair."
Khalil Gibran

~~~

BARE

Let's hear it for bare feet. Do you like to run through grass in your bare feet? Dance on wood floors in your bare feet? Wiggle your bare toes under your blankets? Do you pick up things off the floor with your toes, like my mother and I and your daddy do? I hope so.

Bare feet are a basic, often overlooked, luxury. In some countries people go barefoot out of necessity, because they do not have resources for shoes. But odds are you will have the choice to go barefoot and it is a good choice to make whenever possible.

I took up meditation for awhile. I liked the exercise of it, except for the part of sitting so long my legs went to sleep. One of the good things about meditating was we took off our shoes and I liked the walking meditation best, where we would consciously feel for the floor in our bare feet. We were instructed to deliberately place first our heels and then slowly the balls of our feet and then finally our toes on the worn, warm century-old wooden floors, inhaling through the soles of our feet and up into the souls of ourselves the comfort of mindfulness.

I also liked the lifestyle of meditating, not just the exercise. Extend the concept of baring your feet to the world, to baring yourself to the world and you will belong in a way you will never have belonged to anything before.

117

This may all sound very complicated and pie-in-the-sky to you as a child and it should. For now, don't over-think running barefoot in the rain. Just do it. Feel it. From our balcony, your PaPa and I watch a daddy and his two-year-old son bounce barefoot through puddles whenever it rains, and we cheer them on. How better to experience getting wet than to get thoroughly wet, from the top of your head to the bottom of your feet?

Feel free to leave your shoes at my doorstep anytime.

"Great works are performed not by strength but by perseverance."
Samuel Johnson

~~~

PATIENCE AND THE GLOVES

I promised in another letter to explain what a car's glove compartment was. I also need to write about the virtue of patience and so I am going to try to meld the two.

Long ago when cars were a novelty and just recently born there was no roof to them and driving was an adventure in experiencing the elements. Ladies did not drive, perish the thought, but they would put on their broad-brimmed hats, the better to keep off the sun, and their gloves, again, no sun to freckle the backs of their hands, and they would go for a drive with their favorite drivers.

Somewhere along the early line of vehicle development the idea of a place to store one's gloves was born. Sportier cars needed a firm hand on the slick, very large wheel, and so even the men drivers began wearing gloves, the better to grip and control. Again, there was a need to store the gloves.

So a compartment was designed, long and rather shallow, the shape of those long-ago gloves, and eventually the compartments also began to collect small items other than gloves, because nature abhors a vacuum.

Today I would lay a bet that there are no gloves in anyone's glove compartments, or maybe a tenth of a tenth of a percent of car owners have a glove or two in there. Nowadays, we store our insurance papers in our glove compartments along with a whole lot of other stuff we are content to pretty much never see again.

But the name 'glove compartment' patiently persists. Ah, did you see how cleverly I put in the word 'patiently'?

There is outward patience and true, inward patience, and while one person who seems outwardly calm and willing to wait out a situation may be seething inside, another who is always busy might truly be a still and patient person in their mind. There is no way to tell really who is patient and who is not. Parents have been known to totally fake an impatient moment just to get things moving, when actually, had time or environment allowed it they would have been perfectly happy to just sit and breathe another hour or two.

But it is common knowledge that patience, true patience, is a virtue. The patient live longer, are happier, and have happier families. Impatience is arrogance and breeds discontent, a host of ailments and children who run to escape.

Impatience indicates that the wearer of it considers himself or herself somehow superior, that his or her timetable should trump everyone else's, that his knowledge base is more than adequate, thank you very much, and that he or she should not be subjected to waiting on you to learn your bit.

Arrogant people I have often noticed end up having to put up with a lot more grief, stress, strife and mind-bending bother than those who are humble, kind and yes, patient. The universe has a way of being sure of that, that arrogance sent one way on the impatience route is sent back around with no exit.

Back to the lowly glove compartment. If we could assign a personality to it, we would say it is humble, not at all convinced of its own invincibility, content to just be, perfectly all right with being used for things other than for what it was originally designed, patient in the face of an impatient, rushing world. And we could say, good for it, because how many things are still around, still called by their name and still useful a hundred years or more later? Not many. Only, it would seem, the patient.

~~~

~

"It is more blessed to give than to receive."
Acts 20:35

"No person was ever honored for what he received. He was honored for what he gave."

Calvin Coolidge

~~~

ASSISTANCE

Ask a Girl or Boy Scout sometime if she or he still has a walking stick. A scout walking stick can have some pretty medallions on it that accompany certain badges, but its beauty comes from both its wood and its purpose.

When you hike with your family, and I know you will because you already do, you'll notice people at times carry walking sticks to help them get over a steep spot. As we age we do need a bit of extra help. But the walking stick is a companion, not a dictator. It assists, it doesn't direct.

Some of the most beautiful people I have ever known are assistants. They assist children in learning. They assist the sick. They assist the elderly. They assist those who feel they have no place. They help. They don't do it for the glory or for power. They do it because there is a need and they can fill that need.

Whether or not you grow up to work in a helping profession, you can always find a way to give of yourself. Only in loving and giving can you truly find love. In fact, try to be as anonymous about your assistance as possible. When your father was growing up he and I would look for ways to anonymously help or encourage people. Once we noticed on a daily drive a falling-down house practically hidden behind tall weeds and trees. A car was parked in the drive so we knew it was occupied. We wrote a cheery anonymous note and put it with some home-made cookies and left it in the mailbox. Just a small token as proof that someone somewhere noticed that a person lived there.

When you are young you will be restricted somewhat by what you can do for others. You can't drive yet, you won't have your own money. Actually, this is the time when a true giving spirit is born, when one cannot give money or go. Assisting, giving, sharing should come from the heart, from thoughts and simple actions, not from grandiose gestures. Look around you. Does someone seem sad more often than not? It is not your business to question why, but to reach out as softly and gently and hopefully as anonymously as possible. Does someone need a blanket that you can make? A smile that you can give? A listening ear that you have the time to provide?

Notice around your house, does a parent need a helping hand? Does a sister need a quiet moment? Does the pet need an extra snuggle?

Develop a helping attitude and the world will seem a gentler, more accessible place to you for the rest of your life. Although you will not set out to be a walking stick because someday you will need one yourself, that is the way life works. When you need someone someday, there will be someone for you. A famous and righteous man, Dr. Albert Schweitzer, put it this way: "The ones among you who will be really happy are those who have sought and found how to serve."

The joy of helping others is a joy that is only rivalled, I believe, by the birth of your own child. Seriously, it is such a deep, righteous and holy gift, the gift of giving, that it is practically a requirement for possessing a soul.

Be beautiful, little one. Give of yourself.

~~~

~~~

"Any time women come together with a collective intention, it's a powerful thing. Whether it's sitting down making a quilt, in a kitchen preparing a meal, in a club reading the same book, or around the table playing cards, or planning a birthday party, when women come together with a collective intention, magic happens."
Phylicia Rashad

~~~

SIGNATURE

Your PaPa's great-aunt was a maker of quilts. To say she was a quilt-maker seems inadequate. One needs the 'of' to adequately assign the grandeur a quilter's title deserves. Quilts are wondrous things.

I have been replacing some squares on a quilt she made many, many years ago. The fabric in some of the squares had become so thin it was tearing. As I took apart the seams of the old squares and clumsily, I assure you, since I am no seamstress, sewed on new squares, I took note of the hands that had come before me.

Besides the symphony of colors, patterns and design, quilts are biographies. Whether made by one person or several, stitches are signatures to those who care to look closely. Tiny stitches, uniform stitches? Perhaps a patient person. Thread that doesn't quite match material? Perhaps poor. Squares made of denim, snatches of curtains? Perhaps frugal. Or sentimental.

Stitches that are a conglomerate of direction and size? Perhaps a young quilter. A spiralling design from the middle outward? Perhaps outgoing. A design of predominantly one color? Perhaps a peaceful woman. A design full of vibrant shades? Perhaps carefree.

Consider the purposes of a quilt, so much more than utilitarian: to warm, to keep, to comfort or to indulge in one's love of pattern. To embark on creating a quilt is to have a home in mind, a child in the next room, an aging mother two houses down, newlyweds with no linens, a granddaughter who loves to cuddle. To embark on a quilt is to undertake a masterpiece, a structure of hope.

A quilt is also an investment in a future the quilter will likely never see. Quilts usually outlast their creators. And isn't that the idea of living in the first place? To pass along a legacy, the best of oneself?

I hope for you many quilts of many colors, squares of many nuances, and a signature of many stitches.

"The most courageous act is still to think for yourself.
Aloud."
Coco Chanel

~~~

NO KNIGHT

As a little girl you are very much into princesses. Often your bedtime story is about princesses. This is all good and many strong and smart women have grown up on the fairy tale model, but I would not be doing my job as a grandmother if I didn't tell you there is no knight.

You may be very blessed, as I have been, to have a person come into your life who will help you find yourself. Your PaPa got more than he bargained for when he married me but he was willing to put in the hard work to make it work, and I for him.

Most of the time, though, you will have to depend on yourself to comfort yourself, understand yourself, understand someone else, or make sense of the world. I pray you will believe in God who loves you and guides you, but know you always have the final vote.

You have the free will to make decisions and you and only you will be the one you have to answer to at the end of the day. This may seem like a burden at first, there only being yourself to depend on, but it's not. Knowing this will make you a strong and confident person, a person who is not afraid to make mistakes but who is always willing to learn from them.

I pray you will find someone to love you unconditionally and who will be there for you but even so, don't grow dependent. A partner is a partner, equal.

Stay true to the person you have grown to be and follow your true north. In other words, don't go looking over a distant horizon for a knight on a horse to come save you, a-la-fairy tale style. Saddle your horse yourself, consult your inner compass and ride on out.

"Existence is no more than the precarious attainment of relevance in an intensely mobile flux of past, present, and future."
Susan Sontag

~~~

RELEVANCE

A talented, kind, energetic man was talking to me once on the occasion of his 95th birthday. Friends had been discussing their aches and pains and when I asked him what was the hardest thing about turning 95 I expected a physical complaint to surface.

"Irrelevance," he said instead.

You are too young perhaps to yet understand what it means to not only feel relevant but actually be relevant, but it is a powerful thing. When you feel relevant you are confident. You feel you have a contribution to make to your world. You expect people to listen to you and you listen in return, not afraid of what you might hear.

But when you feel irrelevant you become irrelevant. Unfortunately feelings usually rule our realities. When you are snubbed or overlooked or ignored, or perhaps worst of all, patronized, condescended to, assisted when you didn't require assistance, you begin to feel invisible, unimportant, not valuable.

I hope throughout your life you will be blessed as I have been with many friends who are older than you. You might need a parent figure and you may have one or two but I am not necessarily talking about wisdom shared or guidance provided. I am talking about friendship, about respect, about texture and nuance.

131

Think of all my 95-year old friend has experienced. I know a small part of his experiences and they are fascinating. He has traveled the world, known joy and triumph and heartache. He has come from nothing to something, to nothing and back again. He has wisdom to share, sure, but he also has laughter and talent and ability. For those around him to define him by his age, expect him to be frail (he isn't) or diminished mentally (he isn't) or no longer relatable to the 'real' modern world (he is), is a disservice not only to this human being but to the beings among whom he lives.

Never assume age has anything to do with worth. Your older friends may indeed wear outward or inward scars. Age may be cruel to them. Even so, whether vigorous or slowing or equal to your energy or maybe even superior to your energy, all that matters is that you don't overlook their perspective and their friendship.

In keeping them relevant, you keep yourself relevant. May you never have the occasion to say on a birthday that you are not.

"Joy is not a station you arrive at but a manner of traveling."
Margaret Lee Runbeck

~~~

JOY

I taught first grade Sunday school for over twenty years and ran some large departments during that time. For awhile I was the youngest director the church had and I had to learn how to work alongside teachers much wiser, and yes, quite a bit older than I. We made a fabulous team, my teachers and I, and we saw so many children and their parents pass through our department and come out the other side knowledgeable about their faith and most importantly, joyful.

We had disagreements among ourselves and with the children sometimes, and we had discipline challenges and curriculum challenges. Our first grade department was not perfect. But we had figured out that as long as our passion for children and our faith was with us, we could lean on one another and our classes would be blessed with joy abounding.

They were.

There is a profound difference between joy and happiness, I would tell my first graders. Joy involves putting others before yourself. Joy is deep within, never dissolves and never moves unless you move away from it. In contrast, happiness is an ice cream cone. Temporary. Melting. Not to be depended on. Happiness should not define one's life.

The popular psychology of today tells us to take what makes us happy and turn that into our life's work. There is value in doing with your life what you were born to do, don't get me wrong. But there is true joy in combining your calling, whatever it may be, with doing for others. Instead of only asking yourself what makes me happy, ask yourself, what can I do to bring joy to someone else? In so doing, you will foster joy in yourself.

Joy sees us through tough times, times when we hate the very world we live in, times when we are confused and bewildered, times when we lose those most precious to us. We can have joy, a twin of peace, and still be sad or upset. When you feel the most down, move yourself to do a kindness for another, preferably anonymously. Doing so will water your joy, and joy, like the mustard seed in the Bible story, will grow towering in faith and triumph to shade your soul.

Joy is an attitude. I pray for you strength and diligence in seeking it. When you seek joy, you will find it, and you can travel anywhere with it.

And know that I am always joyfully yours.

"The greatest glory in living lies not in never falling, but in rising every time we fall."
Nelson Mandela

~~~

RESURRECTION

I know of a spiritually and physically beautiful place that burned a decade ago. It was, and still is, an artists' and writers' colony. Buildings burned to the ground. People barely had time to escape the wildfire. Animals were sent running over mountains. Small trees and brush and flowers were burned to nothingness.

But the live oaks, scorched black though they were, had deep roots. Springs dot the landscape. The oaks' roots drank deep from those springs and began to regenerate the trunks and limbs above. Today when I stand in my favorite spot under a sweeping oak limb, overlooking the valley, I note first how many more black chunks of charred bark have been pushed off the tree by growth. Ten years and counting, and as I look up I still can see the black on the trunks. But I also see the green, the tenacious push of limbs and twigs, the life of green leaves.

I came to this scene years after the fire had done its damage but even if no one had told me the land's story I could have seen it for myself. The scars remain and will forever, if nothing else as charcoal bits buried in the dirt. One of my favorite photos I've taken is from the viewpoint of a reviving oak, painfully insisting its way through its burned veneer and stretching, alive with perseverance, toward the valley below and up to the clean skies above.

This is the last letter in this collection and I wanted to leave you with a thought that might surpass all the others that have gone before. You will be burned in life, Cadence. There is no getting around it. You will be hurt. Everyone is burned and we wouldn't be alive if we weren't. Life has built into it flame and smoke and destruction.

But life also has built into it hope and perseverance and growth. You will choose to water your life, your roots, your soul, with art or love or hate or suspicion or doubt or imagination or adventure or impatience or literature or whimsy or song or transcendent mixtures of it all. There are so many springs from which to draw.

Choose your sustenance wisely. Go deep.

Know that as you grow and live and yes, crash and burn, and rise up again and triumph, that many have gone before you and many will follow. You are not alone in this living thing. Living is a glorious endeavor. Wear your scars proudly. Seek to be better than your hurts; indeed, shed your hurts, leave them behind in the dirt. Reach out to the valleys and up to the skies and remember the oaks. Nothing is as bad as it first appears, and nothing on this earth lasts forever. Nothing.

And that is good.

~~

~~~

ACKNOWLEDGEMENTS

I hold a special place in my heart for Lee Bryant Monger, who brainstormed with me at the beginning of this project and over the years since. She has shepherded me through countless big plans and on to their finales.

Many thanks to Robert Willis and Janice Cipriani-Willis for their encouragement and faithful husbandry of the magical Dorland Mountain Arts Colony. Their place, and they as its people, can be found reflected in nearly every letter.

For years of feeding and sheltering me and providing a port from approaching storms my heartfelt thanks to Linda Caldwell, Jana Jones and the Writers' Colony at Dairy Hollow. I'm counting on you to be there for my third book too.

Without fail my husband Forrest has shared my vision for this collection and my love for our granddaughter. He has helped refine the book's goals and expand its perspectives and has often gone it alone while I chased the muse in faraway places. My heart.

There is no more steadfast friend than Elaine Knight, who read the proofs page by page, word by word and knows me so well she could tell, and did, in an instant if at any point I strayed from my true north. I look forward to someday doing the same for her.

Finally, to my son and daughter-in-law and the family and village that backs them, who are raising my granddaughter in the best traditions and modeling responsibility, kindness, humor and unconditional love, my admiration and gratitude. Love you, Trey and Hilary, to the moon and back.

~~~

ABOUT THE AUTHOR

Sherri C. Perry is an author and educator. She lives in Texas with her husband and is the proud grandmother of Cadence. Her poetry and stories have been featured in various literary journals and her first book, *Venn*, a collection of short stories was released in 2014.

~~